SEVEN

Becoming Salt and Light

JENNIFER CRUNKLETON

ISBN 978-1-64458-874-1 (paperback)
ISBN 978-1-64458-875-8 (digital)

Christian Faith Publishing, Inc.
832 Park Avenue
Meadville, PA 16335
www.christianfaithpublishing.com

Printed in the United States of America

CONTENTS

CHAPTER 1

The Relationship

M any, if not all of us, have felt the lack of fulfillment. For me, this has come and gone from as far back as I can remember. Throughout my life, I have been drawn to God but honestly had never really fully invested. As trials in my life arose, I would always find myself turning to him but quickly slipping away after I began to heal. My heart knew where I belonged, but my selfish nature would distance me once more.

There are many reasons our soul begins to desire a relationship with God. It could be a traumatic experience in our life, the feeling of incompleteness, or the desire to know the truth. And with any relationship, it takes selfless efforts to maintain it.

God has always wanted a relationship with us, although we are created with the free will to love and follow him as we desire. God created us to be apart in fulfilling his plan. But from the very beginning of human creation, we have decided to exercise our right of free will, leaving us with a feeling of void.

> The LORD God commanded the man, saying, "From any tree of the garden you may eat freely; but from the tree of the knowledge of good and evil you shall not eat, for in the day that you eat from it you will surely die." (Genesis 2:16–17, NASB)

God created Eve as a companion for Adam, and before Adam and Eve, there were angels; some of which chose not to follow God but worked against him. The plans of evil are to destroy us, and deception makes that task easily done.

> The serpent said to the woman, "You surely will not die! For God knows that in the day you eat from it, your eyes will be opened. And you will be like God, knowing good and evil." When the woman saw that the tree was good for food, and that it was a delight to the eyes, and that the tree was desirable to make one wise. She took from its fruit and ate, and she gave also to her husband with her, and he ate. Then the eyes of both of them were opened, and they knew that they were naked. And they sewed fig leaves together and made themselves loin coverings.
>
> They heard the sound of the LORD God walking in the garden in the cool of the day, and the man and his wife hid themselves from the presence of the LORD God among the trees of the garden. (Genesis 3:4–8, NASB)

God provided Adam guidelines to follow, but the deception of evil prevailed, just as it is easily done today.

> But your iniquities have made a separation between you and your God. And your sins have hidden His face from you so that He does not hear. (Isaiah 59:2, NASB)

Sin separates us from God as the wages of sin is death, but God loves us and offers us grace through his son Jesus Christ.

> But God, being rich in mercy, because of His great love with which He loved us, even when

we were dead in our transgressions, made us alive together with Christ (by grace you have been saved), and raised us up with Him, and seated us with Him in the heavenly places in Christ Jesus, so that in the ages to come He might show the surpassing riches of His grace in kindness toward us in Christ Jesus. For by grace you have been saved through faith; and that not of yourselves, it is the gift of God. (Ephesians 2:4–8, NASB)

Our first step in salvation is to act upon the gift of grace, by believing Jesus is our Lord and savior, and that he was raised from the dead so that we could be saved.

That if you confess with your mouth Jesus as Lord, and believe in your heart that God raised Him from the dead, you will be saved; for with the heart a person believes, resulting in righteous-ness, and with the mouth he confesses, resulting in salvation. (Romans 10:9–10, (NASB)

Nicodemus was a ruler of the Jews, but he believed that Jesus was a teacher from God. Despite the rumors, he chose to experience him for himself. Through this experience, he began to build his rela-tionship with Jesus.

Jesus answered and said to him, "Truly, truly, I say to you, unless one is born again, he cannot see the kingdom of God."

Nicodemus said to Him, "How can a man be born when he is old? He cannot enter a second time into his mother's womb and be born, can he?"

Jesus answered, "Truly, truly, I say to you, unless one is born of water and the Spirit, he can-not enter into the kingdom of God. That which is born of the flesh is flesh, and that which is born of the Spirit is spirit. (John 3:3–6, NASB).

As we begin to build our relationship, evil will try to destroy it. So let no man deceive or divide you, just as Nicodemus. We must examine the truth for ourselves.

> And Jesus answered and said to them, "See to it that no one misleads you." (Matthew 24:4, NASB).

This relationship is personal. It begins with us declaring Jesus as our Lord and having faith in his resurrection, demonstrating our spiritual rebirth to come. Physically, we will lead a new life, following the spirit and choosing to abstain from sin. Although choosing to believe and follow Christ will not eliminate, tests, trials, or evil temptations, as even Jesus was tempted by the devil after being baptized.

(Matthew 3:13–17, NASB)

> Then Jesus arrived from Galilee at the Jordan coming to John, to be baptized by him. But John tried to prevent Him, saying, "I have need to be baptized by You, and do You come to me?" But Jesus answering said to him, "Permit it at this time for in this way it is fitting for us to fulfill all righteousness." Then he permitted Him. After being baptized, Jesus came up immediately from the water; and behold, the heavens were opened, and he saw the Spirit of God descending as a dove and lighting on Him, and behold, a voice out of the heavens said, "This is My beloved Son, in whom I am well-pleased."

(Matthew 4:1–11, NASB)

Then Jesus was led up by the Spirit into the wilderness to be tempted by the devil. And after He had fasted forty days and forty nights, He then became hungry. And the tempter came and said to Him, "If You are the Son of God, command that these stones become bread." But He answered and said, "It is written, 'Man shall not live on bread alone, but on every word that proceeds out of the mouth of god.'"

Then the devil took Him into the holy city and had Him stand on the pinnacle of the temple, and said to Him,

If You are the Son of God, throw Yourself down; for it is written,

"He will command His angels concerning You", and

"On their hands they will bear You up,

So that You will not strike Your foot against a stone."

Jesus said to him, "On the other hand, it is written, 'You shall not put the Lord your God to the test.'"

Again, the devil took Him to a very high mountain and showed Him all the kingdoms of the world and their glory; and he said to Him, "All these things I will give You, if You fall down and worship me."

Then Jesus said to him, "Go, Satan! For it is written, 'you shall worship the Lord your God, and serve Him only.'" Then the devil left Him;

and behold, angels came and began to minister to Him.

* * * * *

We must feed our spirit with his word, just as we nourish our physical body with food and water. Jesus said we cannot live by bread alone but by every word that comes from the mouth of God. Living with the knowledge of the word of God, will help us to be able to turn away or bear such temptations.

James, a servant of God, and Jesus's brother also teaches us about tests, trails, and the temptations we will face. These not only test our free will but build our faith and work our patience.

> Consider it all joy, my brethren, when you encounter various trials, knowing that the testing of your faith produces endurance. And let endurance have its perfect result, so that you may be perfect and complete, lacking in nothing. (James 1:2–4, NASB)

The King James Version uses the word *temptation* instead of trails. Either way, James did not say "if" we face temptations or trails but "when" we face them. By enduring these difficult times with joy in our hearts, knowing God will bring us through them will leave us "lacking in nothing." When we are faced with these difficult times, know that God has promised us that he will always provide us a way out.

> No temptation has overtaken you but such as is common to man; and God is faithful, who will not allow you to be tempted beyond what you are able, but with the temptation will provide the way of escape also, so that you will be able to endure it. (1 Corinthians 10:13, (NASB)

With evil temptations around every corner, history shows we will not always overcome all of them. As we grow in our relationship with him, we will become more aware of these sinful natures and will learn to overcome some, but we will not always succeed. By asking God to forgive us with sincere regret and remorse, we can be forgiven and continue down our path of salvation.

Paul gives us encouragement to maintain our faith in God in all situations. Faith is complete trust or confidence in someone or something. Would you jump out of an airplane, if you did not trust the parachute? Most of us believe the parachute will slow our fall, protecting us as we hit the ground.

It's difficult to have a successful relationship without faith. Without faith, we begin to protect ourselves, showing disbelief and distance.

Remember, there are many false prophets in this world: read his Word and learn with him, pray, have faith in what he has promised, build a strong personal relationship, and let no one come between you.

> What therefore God has joined together, let no man separate. (Mark 10:9, NASB)

Notes:

CHAPTER 2

Obedience

We all have a natural sense of right and wrong, although our own understanding of right and wrong is not perfect. Most of us will try to do the right thing, even if it may be wrong. Having a good understanding of what sin is, will help us grow as a Child of God.

We are curious and creative creatures prone to make mistakes. When sin creeps up, we must know it is sin and learn how to overcome it and salvage our spirit.

Sin is a transgression of the law, and transgression is an act that goes against God's laws, rules, or code of conduct. Iniquity is also sin and is understood as immoral behavior. But sin is easier defined as simply missing the mark of Christlike behaviors.

God provides us with these laws as example of transgressions and iniquities. These laws help to protect us from sin and teach us the way to righteousness.

> Everyone who practices sin also practices lawlessness; and sin is lawlessness. (1 John 3:4, NASB)

God could have easily forced us to live within his righteousness, but his desire, is for us to follow him within our own free will.

> Oh that they had such a heart in them, that they would fear Me and keep all My commandments always, that it may be well with them and with their sons forever! (Deuteronomy 5:29, NASB).

He wants us to love him with all our heart and soul and to desire the knowledge of righteousness without wavering.

> So you shall observe to do just as the LORD your God has commanded you; you shall not turn aside to the right or to the left (Deuteronomy 5:32, NASB).

By walking with the Lord and obeying him, we set a great example for the ones around us so they may prosper as well. God wants nothing less than for all of us to live in eternity with him. He has given us a book of instructions to help guide our paths daily.

> Now it shall come about when he sits on the throne of his kingdom, he shall write for himself a copy of this law on a scroll in the presence of the Levitical priests. It shall be with him and he shall read it all the days of his life that he may learn to fear the LORD his God, by carefully observing all the words of this law and these statutes. (Deuteronomy 17:18-19, NASB)

Although we will not cover the Bible in its entirety or every request of God the verse above states, keep the Word with you and read it all the days of your life. Doing this will continually feed our spirit and help us grow more knowledgeable by the day.

The Ten Commandments are the basic principles of life. Statutes are appointed times, custom, ordinance, or task and Judgments, or either rewards or penalties.

(Exodus 20:1–17, NASB)

Then God spoke all these words, saying,

I am the LORD your God, who brought you out of the land of Egypt, out of the house of slavery.

1. You shall have no other gods before Me.
2. You shall not make for yourself an idol, or any likeness of what is in heaven above or on the earth beneath or in the water under the earth. You shall not worship them or serve them; for I, the LORD your God, am a jealous God, visiting the iniquity of the fathers on the children, on the third and the fourth generations of those who hate Me, but showing loving kindness to thousands, to those who love Me and keep My commandments.
3. You shall not take the name of the LORD your God in vain, for the LORD will not leave him unpunished who takes His name in vain.
4. Remember the Sabbath day, to keep it holy. Six days you shall labor and do all your work, but the seventh day is a Sabbath of the LORD your God; in it you shall not do any work, you or your son or your daughter, your male or your female servant or your cattle or your sojourner who stays with you. For in six days the LORD made the heavens and the earth, the sea and all that is in them, and rested on the seventh day; therefore the LORD blessed the Sabbath day and made it holy.

5. Honor your father and your mother, that your days may be prolonged in the land which the LORD your God gives you.
6. You shall not murder.
7. You shall not commit adultery.
8. You shall not steal.
9. You shall not bear false witness against your neighbor.
10. You shall not covet your neighbor's house; You shall not covet your neighbor's wife, or his male servant, or his female servant, or his ox, or his donkey, or anything that belongs to your neighbor.

* * * * *

The Ten Commandments are like an umbrella to many other instructions that expand upon these basic principles. The Ten Commandments and the expanded details help protect us from sinful and/or painful situations while leading us to the knowledge of righteousness. If we allow even the smallest sinful natures into our lives, it tends to grow and leads us into greater destruction.

The Scribes and Pharisees were two distinct groups during the first century. They seemed to know and understand God's laws, but it appeared they tried to bend them to fit their lifestyles, which lead them to hypocrisy. Hypocrisy is the practice of claiming to have moral standards or beliefs to which one's own behavior does not show.

Woe to you, scribes and Pharisees, hypocrites! For you tithe mint and dill and cummin, and have neglected the weightier provisions of the law: justice and mercy and faithfulness; but these are the things you should have done without neglecting the others. [24] You blind guides, who strain out a gnat and swallow a camel!

> Woe to you, scribes and Pharisees, hypocrites! For you clean the outside of the cup and of the dish, but inside they are full of robbery and self-indulgence. You blind Pharisee, first clean the inside of the cup and of the dish, so that the outside of it may become clean also.
>
> Woe to you, scribes and Pharisees, hypocrites! For you are like whitewashed tombs which on the outside appear beautiful, but inside they are full of dead men's bones and all uncleanness. So you, too, outwardly appear righteous to men, but inwardly you are full of hypocrisy and lawlessness. (Matthew 23:23–28, NASB)

We may be able to hide our true colors from our family, friends, and acquaintances, but we cannot hide from God; he knows our hearts, sinful intentions, thoughts, and plans. When Jesus came, he could easily see through the manipulation of the people. During his time here, he taught us a greater understanding of the law. As God's laws are intended to help people, but throughout history they have often been misquoted and applied. Although many believe with Jesus's new explanation of the laws, that the original Laws are removed, but Jesus expresses a clear understanding of his purpose.

> Do not think that I came to abolish the law or the prophets; I did not come to abolish but to fulfill. For truly I say to you, until heaven and earth pass away, not the smallest letter or stroke shall pass from the Law until all is accomplished. Whoever then annuls one of the least of these commandments, and teaches others to do the same, shall be called least in the kingdom of heaven; but whoever keeps and teaches them, he shall be called great in the kingdom of heaven.
>
> For I say to you that unless your righteousness surpasses that of the scribes and Pharisees,

you will not enter the kingdom of heaven.
Matthew 5:17–20, (NASB)

Jesus did not abolish the laws; he affirmed and defined those principles. He taught us that obedience must be from the heart rather than just technical observance of the letter of the law.

The sixth commandment is "Thou shall not kill," but Jesus tells us that even anger in our heart could put us in danger of judgment.

(Matthew 5:21-22, NASB)

You have heard that the ancients were told, "You shall not commit murder" and "Whoever commits murder shall be liable to the court." But I say to you that everyone who is angry with his brother shall be guilty before the court; and whoever says to his brother, "You good-for-nothing," shall be guilty before the Supreme Court; and whoever says, "You fool," shall be guilty enough to go into the fiery hell.

The seventh commandment is "Thou shall not commit adultery." Jesus again expands on this principle by expressing that even thoughts of lust are sin.

You have heard that it was said, "You shall not commit adultery; but I say to you that everyone who looks at a woman with lust for her has already committed adultery with her in his heart.
Matthew 5:27–28, (NASB)

Our spouses are a gift from God, and should be cherished. God saw it was not good that man should be alone, so he created Eve for Adam, giving us an example to live by. But we can be selfish by nature, and sometimes we may find it easier to look to someone else for our needs and give up on our spouse or just walk away.

All things in life can be hard from time to time, and the good can be easily forgotten when sometimes all we need is a reset and a little effort.

> Some Pharisees came to Jesus, testing Him and asking, "Is it lawful for a man to divorce his wife for any reason at all?"
>
> And He answered and said, "Have you not read that He who created them from the beginning made them male and female, and said, 'For this reason a man shall leave his father and mother and be joined to his wife, and the two shall become one flesh?' So they are no longer two, but one flesh. What therefore God has joined together, let no man separate."
>
> They said to Him, "Why then did Moses command to give her a certificate of divorce and send her away?"
>
> He said to them, "Because of your hardness of heart Moses permitted you to divorce your wives; but from the beginning it has not been this way. And I say to you, whoever divorces his wife, except for immorality, and marries another woman commits adultery." (Matthew 19:3–9, NASB)

Although divorce is permitted in some cases, we should strive to forgive, reconcile, and restore our relationships, rather than easily walking away. God made us to become one with each other and warns us to let no one tear us apart.

We should try and listen to our conscience and to remove ourselves from sinful natures. If we know something is wrong, we should distance ourselves from it. Remember allowing the door to open, leads to a greater destruction.

If your right eye makes you stumble, tear it out
and throw it from you; for it is better for you to
lose one of the parts of your body, than for your
whole body to be thrown into hell. If your right
hand makes you stumble, cut it off and throw it
from you; for it is better for you to lose one of the
parts of your body, than for your whole body to
go into hell. (Matthew 5:2–30, NASB)

We have all fallen short of the glory of the Lord, but our continual growth comes from knowing sin, repenting, and removing ourselves from it.

As a culture, we have become very comfortable telling those little white lies or using God's name in vain. But the truth is anytime we lie our intention is to deceive someone, and the use of God's name in vain is simple dishonoring him. These acts open the door to destruction as when we lie, we often find ourselves having to lie again and again to cover the first lie.

Deception and the inappropriate use of God's name is covered in the Ten Commandments. And Jesus also elaborates on them during his sermon on the mount because those little white lies an inappropriate use of his name is no small matter to God.

The third commandment is "Thou shall not take the name of the Lord thy God in vain." And the ninth commandment is "Thou shall not bear false witness against your neighbor." Bearing false witness means to lie about something or someone.

Again, you have heard that the ancients were
told, "You shall not make false vows, but shall
fulfill your vows to the Lord." But I say to you,
make no oath at all, either by heaven, for it is
the throne of God, or by the earth, for it is the
footstool of His feet, or by Jerusalem, for it is
the city of the great King. Nor shall you make
an oath by your head, for you cannot make one
hair white or black. But let your statement be,

"Yes, yes" or "No, no"; anything beyond these is of evil. (Matthew 5:33–37, NASB)

Let your words be truthful, never having to have to swear especially in God's name. We all know how easy it is to get caught up in sin, even when we are aware of its nature. So keep in mind that others will fail as well. We are taught to turn the other cheek and forgive as we would want to be forgiven.

You have heard that it was said, "An eye for an eye, and a tooth for a tooth." But I say to you, do not resist an evil person; but whoever slaps you on your right cheek, turn the other to him also. If anyone wants to sue you and take your shirt, let him have your coat also. Whoever forces you to go one mile, go with him two. Give to him who asks of you, and do not turn away from him who wants to borrow from you.

You have heard that it was said, "You shall love your neighbor and hate your enemy." But I say to you, love your enemies and pray for those who persecute you. (Matthew 5:38–44, NASB)

When we are hurt by someone, most of us think of revenge, but Jesus teaches us to love and pray for our enemy's. This is not in our human nature, and only Gods can help us love, as he has loved us.

You have heard that it was said, "You shall love your neighbor and hate your enemy." But I say to you, love your enemies and pray for those who persecute you, so that you may be sons of your Father who is in heaven; for He causes His sun to rise on the evil and the good, and sends rain on the righteous and the unrighteous. For if you love those who love you, what reward do you have? Do not even the tax collectors do the same? If you greet only your brothers, what more are you doing than others? Do not even the Gentiles do the same? Therefore you are to be perfect, as your heavenly Father is perfect. (Matthew 5:43–48, NASB)

As verse 46 states, it is easy to love someone that loves you, the challenge is to love the ones that hurt us in spite of the hurt. God can fill us with his Holy Spirit and help us overcome our sinful and selfish natures if we choose. We will never be flawless, but we can strive to be more Christ like in all our actions. Although we are not flawless, it is much easier to see the faults of others, but we are taught not to judge, and examine our own conduct first.

(Matthew 7:1–5, NASB)

Do not judge so that you will not be judged. For in the way you judge, you will be judged; and by your standard of measure, it will be measured to you. Why do you look at the speck that is in your brother's eye, but do not notice the log that is in your own eye? Or how can you say to your brother, "Let me take the speck out of your eye," and behold, the log is in your own eye? You hypocrite, first take the log out of your own eye, and then you will see clearly to take the speck out of your brother's eye.

* * * * *

By examining our own conduct first, we can lovingly forgive and help others.

Goodness is an act of the fruit of the spirit, and is acknowledged during the Sermon on the Mount, but we are warned against doing these good deeds for public approval or acknowledgment.

(Matthew 6:1–4, NASB)

> Beware of practicing your righteousness before men to be noticed by them; otherwise you have no reward with your Father who is in heaven.
>
> So when you give to the poor, do not sound a trumpet before you, as the hypocrites do in the synagogues and in the streets so that they may be honored by men. Truly I say to you, they have their reward in full. But when you give to the poor, do not let your left hand know what your right hand is doing so that your giving will be in secret; and your Father who sees what is done in secret will reward you.

* * * * *

The King James Version uses the term *alms*. Alms can be money, food, donations, handouts, offerings or charity given to others. God wants our goodness to be pure, and not for ulterior motives. It is said that we should not even let our left hand know what your right hand is doing. But in our nature, it is easier to give and be good to others when we are expecting a return, acknowledgment, and or praise. True goodness comes from the heart and is not selfish. We should strive to do these things in private and with no ulterior motive.

We may sometimes reframe from giving for selfish behaviors because we want to hold on to what we have. Although what we have is a gift from God, and he can easily replace it and more if he chooses.

Jesus warns us of worldly treasures, and how they may lead our hearts down the wrong path. From my own personal experience, I can see time and time again, where my desires have taken me in the wrong direction. I would lose focus on God and become distant to his word by getting caught up in worldly possessions, acknowledgements, or achievements.

> Do not store up for yourselves treasures on earth, where moth and rust destroy, and where thieves break in and steal. But store up for yourselves treasures in heaven, where neither moth nor rust destroys, and where thieves do not break in or steal; for where your treasure is, there your heart will be also.
>
> The eye is the lamp of the body; so then if your eye is clear, your whole body will be full of light. But if your eye is bad, your whole body will be full of darkness. If then the light that is in you is darkness, how great is the darkness!
>
> No one can serve two masters; for either he will hate the one and love the other, or he will be devoted to one and despise the other. You cannot serve God and wealth. (Matthew 6:19–24, NASB)

We should test our hearts: where are most of our thoughts, time, and efforts? Remember none of us are perfect, but by redirecting our focus by the second, minute, hour, and day, will help keep us focused in the right direction while building our treasures in heaven, giving us sense of peace and no need for worry.

(Matthew 6:25–34, NASB)

For this reason I say to you, do not be worried about your life, as to what you will eat or what you will drink; nor for your body, as to what you will put on. Is not life more than food, and the body more than clothing?

Look at the birds of the air, that they do not sow, nor reap, nor gather into barns, and yet your heavenly Father feeds them. Are you not worth much more than they? And who of you by being worried can add a single hour to his life? And why are you worried about clothing?

> Observe how the lilies of the field grow; they do not toil nor do they spin, yet I say to you that not even Solomon in all his glory clothed himself like one of these.
>
> But if God so clothes the grass of the field, which is alive today and tomorrow is thrown into the furnace, will He not much more clothe you? You of little faith!
>
> Do not worry then, saying, "What will we eat?" or "What will we drink?" or "What will we wear for clothing?" For the Gentiles eagerly seek all these things; for your heavenly Father knows that you need all these things. But seek first His kingdom and His righteousness, and all these things will be added to you.
>
> So do not worry about tomorrow; for tomorrow will care for itself. Each day has enough trouble of its own.

We must have faith in God to provide as he has promised. But if we choose to take things into our own hands, he may step back and allow us the opportunity to figure it out.

We all at one point in time have experienced the effects of worry and it is a known fact that worry can cause harm to our health, consume our thoughts, and affect how we response to others. It can also cause us to begin to lose our faith in God. We should try and put all things in his hands and be patience with his timing as he and only he knows what is best for us. Although our human nature tends to want to control the situations we face, faith, pray, and fasting can help.

When we are faced with trouble times, we can pray and fast while asking for God's guidance.

Fasting is an act of abstaining from food and is used to seek a closer relationship with God, while prayer is our open door of communication with him. But do these things in private without the acknowledgement of others as these are personal acts in our relationship with him.

(Matthew 6:16–18, NASB)

> Whenever you fast, do not put on a gloomy face as the hypocrites do, for they neglect their appearance so that they will be noticed by men when they are fasting. Truly I say to you, they have their reward in full. But you, when you fast, anoint your head and wash your face so that your fasting will not be noticed by men, but by your Father who is in secret; and your Father who sees what is done in secret will reward you.

* * * * *

Jesus is telling us that when we are connecting with him, in either prayer or fasting, do not allow it to show as our rewards are from him and not in the praise or pity of others.

Fasting can also help remind us that we are not self-sufficient and just how fragile we are without him. As a yearly reminder, God has set aside one day a year for us to fast and reconcile our relationship with him. This appointed time is known as The Day of Atonement. Because no matter how hard we try to stay focused on him, there are things that will distract us. But fasting and prayer can help keep us centered and focused on him and his will.

(Matthew 7:7–12, NASB)

> Ask, and it will be given to you; seek, and you will find; knock, and it will be opened to you. For everyone who asks receives, and he who seeks

finds, and to him who knocks it will be opened. Or what man is there among you who, when his son asks for a loaf, will give him a stone? Or if he asks for a fish, he will not give him a snake, will he? If you then, being evil, know how to give good gifts to your children, how much more will your Father who is in heaven give what is good to those who ask Him!

In everything, therefore, treat people the same way you want them to treat you, for this is the law and the prophets.

* * * * *

Living a Godly life in our world can be trying, but Jesus teaches us to ask for what we need and He will provide. Maybe our prayers are not immediately answered, but I can guarantee you, God has a plan. Although, sometimes his plans may not be as we envisioned.

Our relationships with God will need faith, focus, and follow through, so pray with faith, focus on God's will and follow through with his word, without public approval or acknowledgement.

When you pray, you are not to be like the hypo-crites; for they love to stand and pray in the syna-gogues and on the street corners so that they may be seen by men. Truly, I say to you, they have their reward in full. But you, when you pray, go into your inner room, close your door and pray to your Father who is in secret, and your Father who sees what is done in secret will reward you.

And when you are praying, do not use meaningless repetition as the Gentiles do, for they suppose that they will be heard for their many words. So do not be like them; for your Father knows what you need before you ask Him. Pray, then, in this way:

"Our Father who is in heaven,

"Hallowed be Your name.

"Your kingdom come.

"Your will be done,

"On earth as it is in heaven.

"Give us this day our daily bread.

"And forgive us our debts, as we also have forgiven our debtors.

"And do not lead us into temptation, but deliver us from evil. (For Yours is the kingdom and the power and the glory forever. Amen.)" (Matthew 6:5—13, NASB)

Did you notice in Jesus's prayer he says "forgive us our debts as we forgive our debtors" he is reminding us to forgive others as we would want to be forgiven.

For if you forgive others for their transgressions, your heavenly Father will also forgive you. But if you do not forgive others, then your Father will not forgive your transgressions.(Matthew 6:14–15, NASB)

Forgiveness does not condone the action, but shows love for someone's short comings. We are the salt and light of the earth, but if we make no effort to effect the world around us, how can we share Gods love, good works and glorify him?

(Matthew 5:13–16, NASB)

You are the salt of the earth; but if the salt has become tasteless, how can it be made salty again? It is no longer good for anything, except to be thrown out and trampled underfoot by men.

You are the light of the world. A city set on a hill cannot be hidden; nor does anyone light a lamp and put it under a basket, but on the lampstand, and it gives light to all who are in the house. Let your light shine before men in such a way that they may see your good works, and glorify your Father who is in heaven.

Notes:

CHAPTER 3

The Fruits of the Spirit

The Fruit of the Spirits are nine attributes of a Christian life. Living with these attributes instilled in us will help us demonstrate more Christlike attitudes, even in difficult situations.

(Romans 5:1–5 NASB)

Therefore, having been justified by faith, we have peace with God through our Lord Jesus Christ, through whom also we have obtained our introduction by faith into this grace in which we stand, and we exult in hope of the glory of God. And not only this, but we also exult in our tribulations, knowing that tribulation brings about perseverance; and perseverance, proven character; and proven character, hope, and hope does not disappoint, because the love of God has been poured out within our hearts through the Holy Spirit who was given to us.

* * * * *

On our own it is impossible, but with the Holy Spirit living within us, we can to overcome anything. The closer we get to God, the more we will experience the fruits of the spirit in our lives.

> But the fruit of the Spirit is love, joy, peace, patience, kindness, goodness, faithfulness, gentleness, self-control; against such things there is no law. (Galatians 5:22–23, NASB)

Love is first Fruit of the Spirit and Jesus expressed love as being the great commandment.

> "Teacher, which is the great commandment in the Law?" And He said to him,
> You shall love the lord your god with all your heart, and with all your soul, and with all your mind. This is the great and foremost commandment. The second is like it, "You shall love your neighbor as yourself." On these two commandments depend the whole law and the Prophets. (Matthew 22:36–40, NASB)

Love is undefeatable and unconquerable goodwill that always seeks the highest of the others, no matter what he/she does. It is self-giving that gives freely without expecting anything in return.

The world we live in can encourage selfishness, as it is so easy to get consumed in ourselves and not think or care about others.

Love is sacrificial and was demonstrated by the death of Jesus on the cross. It is not rude or unmannerly and does not act unbecomingly. Love does not insist on things always going our way, for it is not self-seeking; it takes no account of any wrong that has been done to us. It does not rejoice at injustice and unrighteousness but rejoices when right and truth prevail. Love bears up under everything we face, ready to believe the best of every person. It is hope that never fades under any circumstances, and it endures everything without weakening. Love never fails. With true love, all things come naturally.

Joy is not a human-based happiness that comes and goes; it is a spirit-given expression that flourishes best in hard times.

> You also became imitators of us and of the Lord, having received the word in much tribulation with the joy of the Holy Spirit, (1 Thessalonians 1:6, NASB)

The Greek strongly implied that their supernatural joy was due to the Holy Spirit working within them. Having joy during troubled times is difficult, but if we can maintain joy in our hearts during these times, it shows a sign of true joy.

We need to give God control as he knows what is best for us, even when we don't understand. Just for a moment think about the pain that Jesus must have faced his entire life. Is it possible that some of the painful situations we face and how we handle them could be a blessing to us or someone else?

Peace is the presence of God no matter what the conflict. Peace is tranquility, a state of rest, or the opposite of chaos. When a person is dominated by peace, they are calm and have the ability to conduct peacefully in all circumstances. Rather than allowing the difficulties and the pressures of life break us down, we should try to remain calm and poised awaiting the blessings God has promised us. Jesus is described as the Prince of Peace, and will bring peace to our hearts, if we allow it.

> Peace I leave with you; My peace I give to you; not as the world gives do I give to you. Do not let your heart be troubled, nor let it be fearful (John 14:27, NASB).

> Blessed are the peacemakers, for they shall be called sons of God (Matthew 5:9, NASB).

As we depart from our fears and our faith becomes stronger, we can prepare ourselves for an abundant flow of Gods blessings.

Strengthened with all power, according to His glorious might, for the attaining of all steadfastness and patience; joyously (Colossians 1:11, NASB).

Patience is also known as long-suffering in the King James Version (KJV) and is the ability to live with a long fuse while forgiving others, just as God does for us daily. With patience we can accept or tolerate delay, trouble, or suffering without getting angry or upset.

Bearing with one another, and forgiving each other, whoever has a complaint against anyone; just as the Lord forgave you, so also should you. (Colossians 3:13, NASB)

Forgiveness does not excuse or condoning others actions and is not just for the one that has hurt us, but for our own sake as well. We have to recognize no one is perfect and we're all sinners.

Indeed, there is not a righteous man on earth who continually does good and who never sins. (Ecclesiastes 7:20, NASB)

We are strengthened by the Almighty with peace, patience, and joyfulness, forbearing one another in love.

We should try to respond to the hurt with good. Humanly, that is very difficult, so we will need God's help. Try not to focusing on the hurt; instead focus on God's plan for you. As long as we focus on the hurt, the hurt will control us.

Let all bitterness, and wrath, and anger, and clamor, and slander be put away from you, along with all malice. Be kind to one another, tender-hearted, forgiving each other, just as God in Christ also has forgiven you. (Ephesians 4:31–32, NASB)

Gentleness is the quality of being kind, tender, mild-mannered, or soft in action. It does not necessarily mean being nice, one can be nice and not gentle. Nice is defined by the dictionary as being agreeable. Gentleness is showing love for someone by having an outgoing concern for their well-being. In addition to positive affirmations and acts, this can also be presented when demonstrating disciplining.

> The Lord's bond-servant must not be quarrelsome, but be kind to all, able to teach, patient when wronged, with gentleness correcting those who are in opposition, if perhaps God may grant them repentance leading to the knowledge of the truth, and they may come to their senses and escape from the snare of the devil, having been held captive by him to do his will. (2 Timothy 2:24–26, NASB)

Paul is advising Timothy to be gentle with others. Paul also mentions kindness, or in the KJV, meekness in this verse, which indicates that gentleness requires humility. Good guidance should never promote hurt feels, but when done boastfully, proud, or stubborn it can be offensive and or hurtful to others.

(Proverbs 15:1, NASB)

A gentle answer turns away wrath,
But a harsh word stirs up anger.

* * * * *

In the past, I believed that gentleness was a sign of weakness, and others would not listen, unless I was stern in tone and words. But knowing this is an act of the Holy Spirit being active in our lives—and true gentleness requires self-control, thoughtfulness, tact, and the concern of others—now gives it a different perspective in my mind.

Goodness is moral excellence, generosity, integrity, and honesty. The Greek word *agathosune*, translated "goodness," is defined as uprightness of heart and life.

> Beloved, do not imitate what is evil, but what is good. The one who does good is of God; the one who does evil has not seen God. (3 John 1:11, NASB)

Pure goodness comes from the heart; it requires our intentions to have loving motives. For example, doing good for others and not expecting anything in return, giving to the poor or providing for someone, visiting the sick or lonely, volunteering, and praying for others, are all expressions of goodness. God knows our hearts, he wants our actions to be true and not for personal gain.

> Woe to you, scribes and Pharisees, hypocrites! For you are like whitewashed tombs which on the outside appear beautiful, but inside they are full of dead men's bones and all uncleanness. So you, too, outwardly appear righteous to men, but inwardly you are full of hypocrisy and lawlessness. (Matthew 23:27–28, NASB)

The Holy Spirit is sincere love in truthful speech and in the power of God. Acting with true goodness is a selfless act on behalf of others. God gives us goodness through the Holy Spirit, let the Holy Spirit control you, so that our Father can be glorified.

> "Let your light shine before men in such a way that they may see your good works, and glorify your Father who is in heaven" (Matthew 5:16, NASB).

(Hebrews 11:1, NASB)

"Now faith is the assurance of things hoped for, the conviction of things not seen."

* * * * *

True faith will transform our lives, as we will trust God with assurance and confidence. Faith is also physical, shown by service and obedience to God and others. The more we act upon our faith, the stronger our faith will become. Believe in him, and that he is who he says he is and will do that as he has promised.

> As Jesus went on from there, two blind men followed Him, crying out, "Have mercy on us, Son of David!" When He entered the house, the blind men came up to Him, and Jesus said to them, "Do you believe that I am able to do this?" They said to Him, "Yes, Lord." Then He touched their eyes, saying, "It shall be done to you according to your faith."(Matthew 9:27–29, NASB)

The faith that these two men had in Jesus gave them sight and gives us evidence that if we believe, it can be done. But these two men also took action with their faith; they followed him and cried out to him, asking for mercy.

> Even so faith, if it has no works, is dead, being by itself.
> But someone may well say, "You have faith and I have works; show me your faith without the works, and I will show you my faith by my works." (James 2:17–18, NASB)

The more active we are in prayer, study and the Fruits of the Spirit, the more our faith will increase. Having true faith will give us a sense of peace and patience.

Blessed are the gentle, for they shall inherit the earth. (Matthew 5:5, NASB).

But the humble will inherit the land
    And will delight themselves in abundant prosperity (Psalm 37:11, NASB).

Having gentle qualities will allow more peace in our lives. Jesus promises rest if we come unto him, take upon his yoke, and learn from him, being gentle and humble in heart.

Come to Me, all who are weary and heavy-laden, and I will give you rest. Take My yoke upon you and learn from Me, for I am gentle and humble in heart, and you will find rest for your souls. (Matthew 11:28–29, NASB)

He also teaches us how to be gentle throughout the Bible, as he shows obedience, tough love, strong beliefs, but humble ways. We should be humble and gentle with our expressions, having control over our actions, thoughts, and words, especially when we are correcting someone, as this should not promote confrontation.

Gentleness, self-control; against such things there is no law. (Galatians 5:23, NASB)

Daily we are exposed to the sinful natures of the world, but remember God will always provide us a way to escape.

No temptation has overtaken you but such as is common to man; and God is faithful, who will not allow you to be tempted beyond what you are able, but with the temptation will provide the way of escape also, so that you will be able to endure it. (1 Corinthians 10:13, NASB)

Temptation happens to us all, recognizing the situation and people, then removing ourselves from them and praying for God's help are the first steps to overcome these temptations.

All these attributes are accomplished through faith in the power of the Lord—that he can provide fulfillment, and add to goodness, knowledge; to knowledge, self-control; to self-control, perseverance; to perseverance, godliness; to godliness, mutual affection; and to mutual affection, love.

> Now for this very reason also, applying all diligence, in your faith supply moral excellence, and in your moral excellence, knowledge, and in your knowledge, self-control, and in your self-control, perseverance, and in your perseverance, godliness, and in your godliness, brotherly kindness, and in your brotherly kindness, love. (2 Peter 1:5–7, NASB)

Knowing the Fruits of the Spirit will not keep us from failing, but being aware of our own flaws and shortcomings will help us become better at demonstrating them in all situations. We can begin by apologizing quickly after we realize where we fell short. We are human, so failure will happen; but realizing how our actions may have affected us or someone else and sincerely acting upon it will help us to gain self-control in the future.

Notes:

CHAPTER 4

Celebrations

God's laws provide us with the knowledge of sin so we can grow in our righteousness. God has also provided us appointed times, which teach us and keep us focused on his greater plan.

These appointed times are dual in nature as they educate us on both physical and spiritual lessons about our past, present, and future.

> These are the appointed times of the LORD, holy convocations which you shall proclaim at the times appointed for them. 5In the first month, on the fourteenth day of the month at twilight is the LORD's Passover. (Leviticus 23:4–5, NASB)

The Passover is celebrated to remind us of the sacrifice that took place for our salvation. Just as the Israelites were saved by the blood of the lamb over the door post, during the time of exodus. Today, we are saved by the blood of Jesus Christ. We honor this day in remembrance of him and all he has done for us.

> This is good and acceptable in the sight of God our Savior, who desires all men to be saved and to come to the knowledge of the truth. For there

is one God, and one mediator also between God and men, the man Christ Jesus, who gave Himself as a ransom for all, the testimony given at the proper time. (1 Timothy 2:3–6, NASB)

Jesus came in the form of a man, living a holy life, preparing for the perfect sacrifice for our salvation. But before his crucifixion, Jesus shared the Passover with his disciples and tells them to continue to do this in remembrance of him.

And He said to them, "I have earnestly desired to eat this Passover with you before I suffer; for I say to you, I shall never again eat it until it is fulfilled in the kingdom of God." And when He had taken a cup and given thanks, He said, "Take this and share it among yourselves; for I say to you, I will not drink of the fruit of the vine from now on until the kingdom of God comes." And when He had taken some bread and given thanks, He broke it and gave it to them, saying, "This is My body which is given for you; do this in remembrance of Me." And in the same way He took the cup after they had eaten, saying, "This cup which is poured out for you is the new covenant in My blood. (Luke 22:15-20, NASB)

In the Old Testament, sacrifices were held for the forgiveness of sins. But, God saw the sacrifices had become too easy for the people, as they would follow the traditions but were disobedient in their hearts.

"What are your multiplied sacrifices to Me?" Says the lord.
"I have had enough of burnt offerings of rams, And the fat of fed cattle; And I take no

pleasure in the blood of bulls, lambs or goats.
(Isaiah 1:11, NASB)

The New Testament differs from the Old Testament by removing those sacrifices with one final sacrifice, Jesus Christ. Just as the sins were covered in the Old Testament by the blood of sacrifices, one final loss of life saves ours. But let not your heart become ungracious as shown in history. God wants our hearts to desire to follow him, while trying to restrain from sin and not taking for granted the sacrifice that has been given for us.

(Hebrews 10:26, NASB)

For if we go on sinning willfully after receiving the knowledge of the truth, there no longer remains a sacrifice for sins.

* * * * *

I cannot even imagine what Christ must have went through to offer us salvation, and I would never want to take advantage of that, but daily I see my worldly natures arise. We have to keep ourselves focused on his will and desires for us.

Clean out the old leaven so that you may be a new lump, just as you are in fact unleavened. For Christ our Passover also has been sacrificed. (1 Corinthians 5:7, NASB)

Unleavened in Greek means uncorrupted and leaven is wrong or evil doing. Our soul needs to be cleansed from corruption, and the resurrection of Jesus allows that process to take place.

In the first month, on the fourteenth day of the month at evening, you shall eat unleavened bread,

until the twenty-first day of the month at evening. Seven days there shall be no leaven found
in your houses; for whoever eats what is leavened,
that person shall be cut off from the congregation
of Israel, whether he is an alien or a native of the
land. You shall not eat anything leavened; in all
your dwellings you shall eat unleavened bread.
(Exodus 12:18–20, NASB)

The observance of unleavened bread can be cleansing, educat-
ing, and a reminder of just how easily we can be consumed by sin.

Leaven as known today, is a rising agent used in most bread. An
example is how a small loaf of dough can double or triple in size, just
by adding a little leaven.

Being obedient during this appointed time and removing leaven
from our diet gives us a great example of how sin is everywhere and
just a small amount can be destructive to our lives. It realigns our
thoughts and makes us more aware of our surrounding, while realizing our need for repentance of our sins and symbolizes the removal
of our sins through Jesus.

Therefore, let us celebrate the feast, not with old
leaven, nor with the leaven of malice and wickedness, but with the unleavened bread of sincerity
and truth. (1 Corinthians 5:8, NASB)

Jesus's sacrifice made it possible for us to remove the old leaven.
Observing this appointed time can help raise our awareness of all the
evil around us, and how we always need to look into details of the
ingredients in our nature. Alone we may be confused, but with the
Holy Spirit living within us, our eyes can become open.

Pentecost is held fifty days after the Passover; it is also identified
as the Feast of Harvest and the Feast of Weeks. It is observed during
harvest season and teaches us about the chosen ones and the gift of
his Holy Spirit.

But now Christ has been raised from the dead, the first fruits of those who are asleep. (1 Corinthians 15:20, NASB)

Jesus was the first fruit, the beginning of harvesting souls by resurrection. After his resurrection and during Pentecost, he poured out the Holy Spirit for all that choose to receive it.

(Acts 2:1–4, NASB)

When the day of Pentecost had come, they were all together in one place. And suddenly there came from heaven a noise like a violent rushing wind, and it filled the whole house where they were sitting. And there appeared to them tongues as of fire distributing themselves, and they rested on each one of them. And they were all filled with the Holy Spirit and began to speak with other tongues, as the Spirit was giving them utterance.

* * * * *

The Holy Spirit is offered to all of us, regardless of our language or culture. By accepting God's Spirit and allowing it to led us, we are sanctified and set apart as Christians. If we allow it, God's Holy Spirit will empower us with the desire to obey him with a sound mind and the will to discern the truth.

"For all who are being led by the Spirit of God,
these are sons of God" (Romans 8:14, NASB).

In the Old Testament God provides great analogies of what he expect from the firstfruit using the terms like, *without blemish, fine flour, oil,* and *frankincense* to make a *sweet savor* made with *unleavened* and *seasoned with salt.* Jesus fulfilled all of these attributes and became the firstfruit of the resurrections to come. These details teach us to be our best while removing sin and showing his presents in our lives.

> For since by a man came death, by a man also came the resurrection of the dead. For as in Adam all die, so also in Christ all will be made alive. But each in his own order: Christ the first fruits, after that those who are Christ's at His coming. (1 Corinthians 15:21–23, NASB)

> And He will send forth His angels with A great trumpet and they will gather together His elect from the four winds, from one end of the sky to the other (Matthew 24:31, NASB).

Trumpets are used throughout the Bible as warnings, calling for a gathering, and a sound of peace.

> "For the Lord Himself will descend from heaven with a shout, with the voice of the archangel and with the trumpet of God, and the dead in Christ will rise first" (1 Thessalonians 4:16, NASB).

During the Feast of Trumpets, we are reminded of Jesus's return and the beginning of the resurrections to come.

> Again the LORD spoke to Moses, saying, "Speak to the sons of Israel, saying, 'In the seventh month on the first of the month you shall have a rest, a reminder by blowing of trumpets, a holy convocation (Leviticus 23:23–24, NASB).

God's plan for perfection will come to pass. This memorial, a holy convocation, reminds and teaches us his plan, warning us of the destruction and deceit that will face before it is fulfilled.

> For if the bugle produces an indistinct sound, who will prepare himself for battle? (1 Corinthians 14:8, NASB)

We need to educate ourselves, so that we can discern spiritual direction and understand the battles we will face. In a twinkling of an eye, the end can come and we need to be ready.

> In a moment, in the twinkling of an eye, at the last trumpet; for the trumpet will sound, and the dead will be raised imperishable, and we will be changed. (1 Corinthians 15:52, NASB)

Overcoming the battles of life will take removing obstacles in our relationship with God. The Day of Atonement represents our reconciliation with God. The process on our part needs humility and honesty with true repentance while fasting and praying to draw us closer to God.

Atonement means satisfaction or reparation for a wrong, which has been accomplished through the life, suffering, and sacrifice of Jesus Christ.

> For the life of the flesh is in the blood, and I have given it to you on the altar to make atonement for your souls; for it is the blood by reason of the life that makes atonement. (Leviticus 17:11, NASB)

The shedding of Jesus's blood was the greatest offer that could ever be given for our sins. Honoring Atonement allows us to focus on Jesus as he gave his life to atone for all of our sins. It is a time to give thanks, praise, to humble ourselves, seek repentance, cleans our soul, and restore our relationship with God.

> Much more then, having now been justified by His blood, we shall be saved from the wrath of

God through Him. For if while we were enemies we were reconciled to God through the death of His Son, much more, having been reconciled, we shall be saved by His life. And not only this, but we also exult in God through our Lord Jesus Christ, through whom we have now received the reconciliation. (Romans 5:9–11, NASB).

Satan has influenced every one of us to walk in the ways of disobedience or ignorance, and as we grow closer to God he will try and separate us.

In which you formerly walked according to the course of this world, according to the prince of the power of the air, of the spirit that is now working in the sons of disobedience. (Ephesians 2:2, NASB)

There will come a time when Satan is lock away, so that he cannot deceive the world.

(Revelation 20:1–3, NASB)

Then I saw an angel coming down from heaven, holding the key of the abyss and a great chain in his hand. And he laid hold of the dragon, the serpent of old, who is the devil and Satan, and bound him for a thousand years; and he threw him into the abyss, and shut *it* and sealed *it* over him, so that he would not deceive the nations any longer, until the thousand years were completed; after these things he must be released for a short time.

* * * * *

During this appointed time, we should fast drawing us closer to him and his righteousness, while helping us remember how temporary our physical existence is and how we need him to sustain us daily. We should also remember his promise to lock Satan away for a thousand years. I believe this time is given, for all to have an opportunity to know the truth without the deceit and lust of the world.

The Feast of Tabernacles or Feast of Ingathering is appointed at the end of harvest time and symbolizes the great ingathering of believers.

> Speak to the sons of Israel, saying, 'On the fifteenth of this seventh month is the Feast of Booths for seven days to the LORD. (Leviticus 23:34, NASB)

While celebrating this appointed time in the Old Testament, the Israelites would leave their homes and built temporary dwelling places to live in while honoring this feast. This reminded them of their release from slavery and their dwelling in booths when God brought them out of Egypt.

> You shall thus celebrate it as a feast to the LORD for seven days in the year. It shall be a perpetual statute throughout your generations; you shall celebrate it in the seventh month. You shall live in booths for seven days; all the native-born in Israel shall live in booths, so that your generations may know that I had the sons of Israel live in booths when I brought them out from the land of Egypt. I am the LORD your God. (Leviticus 23:41–43, NASB)

This celebration can also be a great example of the restoration process to come. As with booths our temporary dwellings which are our physical body is a holding place for better things to come, if we choose. Jesus is coming back to restore us and the world we know now.

(2 Corinthians 5:1–2, NASB)

For we know that if the earthly tent which is our house is torn down, we have a building from God, a house not made with hands, eternal in the heavens. For indeed in this house we groan, longing to be clothed with our dwelling from heaven.

* * * * *

Being part of the first resurrection is a great honor, as Satan will be lock away and those that are raised will reign with Jesus for one thousand years.

The rest of the dead did not come to life until the thousand years were completed. This is the first resurrection. Blessed and holy is the one who has a part in the first resurrection; over these the second death has no power, but they will be priests of God and of Christ and will reign with Him for a thousand years. (Revelation 20:5–6, NASB)

The gate to heaven is narrow, and all will not find that path as the gate to destruction is broad and easier found.

(Matthew 7:13–14, NASB)

Enter through the narrow gate; for the gate is wide and the way is broad that leads to destruction, and there are many who enter through it. For the gate is small and the way is narrow that leads to life, and there are few who find it.

Living for God may not always popular or comfortable, but choosing to follow him now will have greater rewards in the future.

Not everyone who says to Me, "Lord, Lord," will enter the kingdom of heaven, but he who does the will of My Father who is in heaven will enter. Many will say to Me on that day, "Lord, Lord, did we not prophesy in Your name, and in Your name cast out demons, and in Your name perform many miracles?" And then I will declare to them, "I never knew you; depart from me, you who practice lawlessness." (Matthew 7:21–23, NASB)

Jesus reminds us all, that if we thirst, we must come to him and drink, and if we believe in him, our belly will flow rivers of living water.

Now on the last day, the great day of the feast, Jesus stood and cried out, saying, "If anyone is thirsty, let him come to Me and drink. He who believes in Me, as the Scripture said, 'From his innermost being will flow rivers of living water.'" (John 7:37–38, NASB)

Before it is all fulfilled, there will come, "the last day, that great day." This day is sometimes referred to as Judgment Day.

(Revelation 20:11–15, NASB)

Then I saw a great white throne and Him who sat upon it, from whose presence earth and heaven fled away, and no place was found for them. And I saw the dead, the great and the small, standing before the throne, and books were opened; and another book was opened, which is the book of life; and the dead were judged from the things which were written in the books, according to their deeds. And the sea gave up the dead which were in it, and death and Hades gave up the dead which were in them; and they were judged, every one of them according to their deeds. Then death and Hades were thrown into the lake of fire. This is the second death, the lake of fire. And if anyone's name was not found written in the book of life, he was thrown into the lake of fire.

* * * * *

The final judgment will complete God's plan of salvation. But God does not want to lose any of his children and his promises are true.

"The Lord is not slow about His promise as some count slowness, but is patient toward you, not wishing for any to perish but for all to come to repentance" (2 Peter 3:9, NASB).

By walking and loving him with all our heart, we can look forward to the restoration of all that he has promised us.

Now, Israel, what does the LORD your God require from you, but to fear the LORD your God, to walk in all His ways and love Him, and to serve the LORD your God with all your heart and with all your soul, and to keep the LORD's commandments and His statutes which I am commanding you today for your good? (Deuteronomy 10:12–13, NASB)

If we choose, he will give us a new heart filled with his spirit, so our walk with him can be fulfilled.

Moreover, I will give you a new heart and put a new spirit within you; and I will remove the heart of stone from your flesh and give you a heart of flesh. I will put My Spirit within you and cause you to walk in My statutes, and you will be careful to observe My ordinances. Ezekiel 36:26–27, NASB)

God has invited us to remember and rejoice in all that he has done, is doing, and will do in our future. It's up to us to take part in his celebrations.

Notes:

CHAPTER 5

Our Temple

We are wonderfully created in God's image, and God makes no mistakes.

> "God created man in His own image, in the image of God He created him; male and female He created them" (Genesis 1:27, NASB).

By free will, we have all fallen from the perfection of God. But when we sin against our body, we are sinning against the temple that houses the Holy Spirit.

> Do you not know that you are a temple of God and that the Spirit of God dwells in you? If any man destroys the temple of God, God will destroy him, for the temple of God is holy, and that is what you are. (1 Corinthians 3:16–17, NASB)

When our body receives the Holy Spirit, it is a gift from God, and he expects us to honor it and use it properly.

Our culture is full of abuse to our temples. It could be high-stressed environments, the foods we eat, lack of rest and/or exercise, drugs or alcohol, sexual abuse, worry, etc. Some of these could cause, heart failure, food-borne illnesses, overdose, loss of bodily functions, distress, or STDs. We will not cover all areas of bodily abuse; but as your journey begins with God, he will revile more than you could have ever image.

> Do you not know that your bodies are members of Christ? Shall I then take away the members of Christ and make them members of a prostitute? May it never be! Or do you not know that the one who joins himself to a prostitute is one body with her? For He says, "the two shall become one flesh." But the one who joins himself to the Lord is one spirit with Him. Flee immorality. Every other sin that a man commits is outside the body, but the immoral man sins against his own body. Or do you not know that your body is a temple of the Holy Spirit who is in you, whom you have from God, and that you are not your own? For you have been bought with a price: therefore glorify God in your body. (1 Corinthians 6:15–20, NASB)

Many sins defile our bodies and mock the temple of the Holy Spirit that dwells within us. As we learned from Jesus's sermon on the mount, sexual sin is not only physical, but the thoughts of acting those desires out can cause destruction alone.

Some may ask why I did not physically do it? I believe that although you can't get an STD while withholding from the physical sexual sin, it affects our minds and opens the door to greater destruction.

All through the Bible, God teaches us about the different acts of sexual sin; some of these include harlotry, incest, fornication, and adultery. Sexual sins are very common and somewhat accepted in our culture today. It appears to have always been a weakness from the beginning, as Paul warns us not to let our lustful thoughts or actions control us.

(1 Thessalonians 4:1–8, NASB)

Finally then, brethren, we request and exhort you in the Lord Jesus, that as you received from us instruction as to how you ought to walk and please God (just as you actually do walk), that you excel still more. For you know what commandments we gave you by the authority of the Lord Jesus. For this is the will of God, your sanctification; that is, that you abstain from sexual immorality; that each of you know how to possess his own vessel in sanctification and honor, not in lustful passion, like the Gentiles who do not know God; and that no man transgress and defraud his brother in the matter because the Lord is the avenger in all these things, just as we also told you before and solemnly warned you. For God has not called us for the purpose of impurity, but in sanctification. So, he who rejects this is not rejecting man but the God who gives His Holy Spirit to you.

Some may feel if they have already sinned by thinking about it, they may as well go ahead with the action. But acting out sinful desires only makes things worse, as we begin to excuse our sinful thoughts and ignore our conscience.

Satan will try and confuse us, although God has put his spirit within us, making us aware of sin and deceit. But we have to listen to our conscience and follow our discernment.

Most of us have been taught that drugs and alcohol can be harmful to our health, although many think it's harmless. Thousands have abused these substances and still appear to succeed in school, sports, and everyday life, so it is easy for us to dismiss the warnings. But despite these perceptions, even casual drug and alcohol use can have devastating consequences.

Do you remember one of the Fruits of the Spirit being self-control? If we are under the influence, do we really have full control of our actions? Although we are fully responsible for our actions, do we respond in the same manner, as if we were not under the influence?

Many have claimed to use drugs and or alcohol to enhance their spirituality, and others say the Bible doesn't say anything about drugs. But it does tell us to be filled with the Holy Spirit, having self-control and not to be inebriated.

> "And do not get drunk with wine, for that is dissipation, but be filled with the Spirit" (Ephesians 5:18, NASB).

During biblical times to my knowledge, most common drugs were nonexistent in their form today, like LSD, heroin, Ecstasy, cocaine, and methamphetamine. But the truth is drugs and alcohol affects our minds and bodies, causing us to loose self-control.

> But I say, walk by the Spirit, and you will not carry out the desire of the flesh. (Galatians 5:16, NASB).

We all have sinful natures, but we cannot allow it to consume or control us. We have to listen to conscience and follow the Holy Spirit while removing the works of the flesh.

> Now the deeds of the flesh are evident, which are: immorality, impurity, sensuality, idolatry, sorcery, enmities, strife, jealousy, outburst anger, disputes, dissensions, factions, envying, drunkenness, carousing, and things like these, of which I forewarn you, just as I have forewarned you, that those who practice such things will not inherit the kingdom of God. (Galatians 5:19–21, NASB)

God knows even the smallest sins can consume us, while causing pain and destruction. We must avoid these types of behaviors and focus on building our relationship with God.

> Therefore be careful how you walk, not as unwise men but as wise, making the most of your time, because the days are evil. So then do not be foolish, but understand what the will of the Lord is. (Ephesians 5:15–17, NASB)

Feeding our souls daily with his word will help us overcome some of the evil temptations of this world just as we feed our physical bodies to sustain our health. Our bodies need a healthy consumption of food, along with proper sleep, exercise, and appropriate social activities. That's why God established a dietary plan for us and has instructed us on proper body nourishment from the beginning.

> Then God said, "Behold, I have given you every plant yielding seed that is on the surface of all the earth, and every tree which has fruit yielding seed; it shall be food for you. (Genesis 1:29, NASB)

It appears that he is telling us, that the plants and fruits that bear seeds are good for consumption.

> The LORD God planted a garden toward the east, in Eden; and there He placed the man whom He had formed. Out of the ground the LORD God caused to grow every tree that is pleasing to the sight and good for food; the tree of life also in the midst of the garden, and the tree of the knowledge of good and evil.(Genesis 2:8–9, NASB)

Although God created all, he warned us that some creations are not for consumption, like the tree of good and evil. God told Adam and Eve that by eating of this tree, they would surely die.

"But from the tree of the knowledge of good and evil you shall not eat, for in the day that you eat from it you will surely die" (Genesis 2:17, NASB).

The lust of the flesh will lead us to death if we allow it. By making the choice of eating from this forbidden tree, sin, pain, and destruction came unto the whole world. But God did not and does not give up on us; he consistently presses forward to guide us even though our choices could bring us repercussions or death.

Although I have not found detailed instruction on meat until the time of Moses, it appears the knowledge was at hand, as Noah new the difference between clean and unclean meats as he prepared the ark.

(Genesis 7:1–3, NASB)

Then the LORD said to Noah, "Enter the ark, you and all your household, for you alone I have seen to be righteous before Me in this time. You shall take with you of every clean animal by sevens, a male and his female; and of the animals that are not clean two, a male and his female; also of the birds of the sky, by sevens, male and female, to keep offspring alive on the face of all the earth.

Just as with the plants and fruits, God gave us a detailed dietary plan for meat consumption.

(Leviticus 11:1–8, NASB)

The LORD spoke again to Moses and to Aaron, saying to them, "Speak to the sons of Israel, saying, 'These are the creatures which you may eat from all the animals that are on the earth. Whatever divides a hoof, thus making split hoofs, and chews the cud, among the animals, that you may eat. Nevertheless, you are not to eat of these, among those which chew the cud, or among those which divide the hoof: the camel, for though it chews cud, it does not divide the hoof, it is unclean to you. Likewise, the Shaphan, for though it chews cud, it does not divide the hoof, it is unclean to you; the rabbit also, for though it chews cud, it does not divide the hoof, it is unclean to you; [7] and the pig, for though it divides the hoof, thus making a split hoof, it does not chew cud, it is unclean to you. You shall not eat of their flesh nor touch their carcasses; they are unclean to you.

The basic qualities for healthy meats are the animals that have both split hooves and chew their cud. For example, a cow has eight stomachs. They chew their cud and have split hooves. Have you ever noticed that when you see a cow, it always seems to be chewing something? Cows chew their food twice in order to properly digest it. Chewing cud is an indicator of a healthy animal; healthy animal will produce more milk or have a higher production of muscle. Animals who do not chew their cud could have digestive issues, causing a lack of nutrients or improper release of toxins. Other examples of animals that chew their cud include deer, camels, buffalo, goats, sheep, and giraffes; but keep in mind that they should also have split hooves. The camel and the giraffe do not, so they would not be a healthy meat for our consumption. However, the pig does have split hooves but does not chew its cud.

These you may eat, whatever is in the water: all that have fins and scales, those in the water, in the seas or in the rivers, you may eat. But whatever is in the seas and in the rivers that does not have fins and scales among all the teeming life of the water, and among all the living creatures that are in the water, they are detestable things to you, and they shall be abhorrent to you; you may not eat of their flesh, and their carcasses you shall detest. Whatever in the water does not have fins and scales is abhorrent to you. Leviticus 11:9–12, NASB)

Seafood lovers should look for fish that have both fins and scales. Scales are part of the fish's integumentary system, and the integumentary system acts to protect the fish from various things. Both the split hooves and the fins seem to be for mobility and defense but could play a larger role that I do not understand.

(Leviticus 11:13–30, NASB)

These, moreover, you shall detest among the birds; they are abhorrent, not to be eaten: the eagle and the vulture and the buzzard, and the kite and the falcon in its kind, every raven in its kind, and the ostrich and the owl and the sea gull and the hawk in its kind, and the little owl and the cormorant and the great owl, and the white owl and the pelican and the carrion vulture, and the stork, the heron in its kinds, and the hoopoe, and the bat.

All the winged insects that walk on all fours are detestable to you. Yet these you may eat among all the winged insects which walk on all fours: those which have above their feet jointed legs with which to jump on the earth. These of them you may eat: the locust in its kinds, and the devastating locust in its kinds, and the cricket in its kinds, and the grasshopper in its kinds. But all other winged insects which are four-footed are detestable to you.

By these, moreover, you will be made unclean: whoever touches their carcasses becomes unclean until evening, and whoever picks up any of their carcasses shall wash his clothes and be unclean until evening. Concerning all the animals which divide the hoof but do not make a split hoof, or which do not chew cud, they are unclean to you: whoever touches them becomes unclean. Also whatever walks on its paws, among all the creatures that walk on all fours, are unclean to you; whoever touches their carcasses becomes unclean until evening, and the one who picks up their carcasses shall wash his clothes and be unclean until evening; they are unclean to you.

Now these are to you the unclean among the swarming things which swarm on the earth: the mole, and the mouse, and the great lizard in its kinds, and the gecko, and the crocodile, and the lizard, and the sand reptile, and the chameleon.

These verses give us a clear example of the types of fowl, insect, and small animals that are unhealthy for our consumption. Although it does not expand a lot on the healthier fowl and insect, there seems to be a pattern with what we have read. It appears we should steer clear of the type of animal that are known for eating other dead animals or cleaning their surroundings. That would make since being they could be consuming disease without the ability for it to process out of their bodies. We then could consume those diseases or germs, causing us sickness.

Now every swarming thing that swarms on the earth is detestable, not to be eaten. Whatever crawls on its belly, and whatever walks on all fours, whatever has many feet, in respect to

every swarming thing that swarms on the earth,
you shall not eat them, for they are detestable.
(Leviticus 11:41–42, NASB)

This is the law regarding the animal and the bird,
and every living thing that moves in the waters
and everything that swarms on the earth, to make
a distinction between the unclean and the clean,
and between the edible creature and the creature
which is not to be eaten. (Leviticus 11:46–47,
NASB)

In the King James Version (KJV) God calls unclean consumption abominations, this translation uses the word *detestable* or *abhorrent*. All of these have a meaning of dislike, disgust, repulsive etc. They are used throughout the Bible explain many different types of sin, like dishonesty, pride, homosexuality, and more. They are known as unacceptable and intolerable things to God. But he does not stop here, he also warns us of the consumption of both fat and blood.

It is a perpetual statute throughout your generations in all your dwellings: you shall not eat any
fat or any blood. (Leviticus 3:17, NASB)

Our culture today sees many of these abominations acceptable; but as we look at today's medical studies and the world around us, it may help us understand why God instructed us to sustain from them.

And He said to them, "You are those who justify
yourselves in the sight of men, but God knows
your hearts; for that which is highly esteemed
among men is detestable in the sight of God."
(Luke 16:15, NASB)

There are numerous ways we can defile our temple and debates all around those topics. But as we build on our relationship with God and allow him to guide us through the research, he will reveal the truth to us.

Notes:

CHAPTER 6

Testify

Have you ever wondered what our purpose is or why God created us? I believe we'll not truly understand the entire purpose of his plan during our time on earth. But I do believe, we all were created to fulfill a part of his plan during our time here.

We saw where we are created in his image, but did you realize that God created us numbering the hairs on our head?

> "Indeed, the very hairs of your head are all numbered. Do not fear; you are more valuable than many sparrows" (Luke 12:7, NASB).

God numbered the hairs on our head and expressed how valuable we are to him, so there must be a purpose for us. We know that we are to love him with all our heart, soul, and mind as Jesus commanded.

> "Teacher, which is the great commandment in the Law?" And He said to him, "You shall love the lord your God with all your heart, and with all your soul, and with all your mind. This is the great and foremost commandment. The second is like it, You shall love your neighbor as your-

self. On these two commandments depend the whole Law and the Prophets." (Matthew 22:36-40, NASB)

As we learned in chapter 3, love is self-giving freely and sacrificial. It is not rude and does not insist on things going our way and rejoices when right and truth prevail. Love can sometimes be hard, but God has promised us all things work together for the good of them that love him.

> And we know that God causes all things to work together for good to those who love God, to those who are called according to His purpose. (Romans 8:28, NASB)

Now we may not be one of the twelve apostles, but God has called us for a purpose. He tells us to follow him and he will make us fishers of men.

> And He said to them, "Follow Me, and I will make you fishers of men" (Matthew 4:19, NASB).

He has offered us His Holy Spirit, and if received, we should not allow our salt to lose its flavor or our light to be hidden.

(Matthew 5:13–16, NASB)

> You are the salt of the earth; but if the salt has become tasteless, how can it be made salty again? It is no longer good for anything, except to be thrown out and trampled underfoot by men.
> You are the light of the world. A city set on a hill cannot be hidden; nor does anyone light a lamp and put it under a basket, but on the lampstand, and it gives light to all who are in the

house. Let your light shine before men in such a way that they may see your good works, and glorify your Father who is in heaven.

We are called to walk in his spirit and not in the lust of the world, shining outward as an example for others, sharing and showing our faith to the world.

(Romans 12:1–2, NASB)

Therefore I urge you, brethren, by the mercies of God, to present your bodies a living and holy sacrifice, acceptable to God, which is your spiritual service of worship. And do not be conformed to this world, but be transformed by the renewing of your mind, so that you may prove what the will of God is, that which is good and acceptable and perfect.

God gave us the Fruits of the Spirit to provide us with examples of showing salt and light; He also provides examples of conforming to the world and the evils that are common to human nature.

Now the deeds of the flesh are evident, which are: immorality, impurity, sensuality, idolatry, sorcery, enmities, strife, jealousy, outbursts of anger, disputes, dissensions, factions, envying, drunkenness, carousing, and things like these, of which I forewarn you, just as I have forewarned you, that those who practice such things will not inherit the kingdom of God. (Galatians 5:19–21, NASB)

Being filled with all unrighteousness, wickedness, greed, evil; full of envy, murder, strife, deceit, malice; they are gossips, slanderers, haters of God, insolent, arrogant, boastful, inventors of evil, disobedient to parents, without understanding, untrustworthy, unloving, unmerciful. (Romans 1:29–31, NASB)

We need to understand and remove these actions from our lives, while filling it with the Fruits of the Spirit. So how do we overcome the bouts of evil in this world when so many of them are completely acceptable in our society?

We have to turn to God for help, as we will get caught up in some of these, no matter how hard we are trying to live righteous. That is why Jesus had to save us; we cannot do this alone. So as we are trying to lead by example, while teaching others, we must be knowledgeable of these areas.

Backstabbing or backbiting is speaking spitefully or being slanderous about one person to another, and being spiteful is to show malicious or ill will or having the desire to hurt someone else.

How about being proud? This attribute possesses a high or unreasonable conceit of one's own excellence and boasters are those who boast, or brag about themselves.

A Covenant-breaker also known as heresy, fractions, or haters of God, are those who hear and yet rebelled while implacable is being unforgiving, relentless, without mercy, cruel, or harsh.

Let us behave properly as in the day, not in carousing and drunkenness, not in sexual promiscuity and sensuality, not in strife and jealousy(Romans 13:13, NASB).

Inventing evil things like rioting, taking part in a violence or public disturbance, wild parties, or behaving in an unrestrained ways can lead us down a destructive path. You can sometimes see these behaviors in an inebriated person, as drunkenness is the state of being intoxicated, causing us to lose control or act different that we would normally.

Sexual immorality is illicit intercourse, known as adultery, prostitution, sexual relations between unmarried individuals (also known as fornication), homosexuality, and bestiality. Adultery is voluntary sexual intercourse between a married person and a person who is not his or her spouse. Lustful pleasures are an act of sexual immorality, also known as acting filthy, flirtatious, indicating sexual interest, or lustfulness of photographs, porn, etc.

Envying is the feeling of displeasure produced by witnessing or hearing about the prosperity of another. Hatred is the feeling of one who hates or dislikes another. Dissension, quarreling, or hostility is a bitter sometimes violent conflict or anger with someone. Gossip is casual or unconstrained conversation or reports about other people, typically involving details that are not confirmed as being true. Deceit is the action or practice of deceiving someone by concealing or misrepresenting the truth. Division or insolent is conducting or speaking with disrespect, inciting people to rebel against the authority or the action of separating something.

Uncleanness is lacking in moral, spiritual, or physical cleanliness; and unrighteousness is failing to adhere to moral principles and laws while variance is being inconsistent.

Idolatry is the worship of idols or something other than God. Sorcery also known as witchcraft is the art or practice of magic, the use of spells and the invocation of spirits.

Murder is the unlawful killing with malice aforethought of another human. Wickedness is delighting in evil natures and or practicing it.

Emulation or selfish ambitions is the effort or desire to match or surpass a person's achievement, typically by imitation. Greed is the excessive desire to acquire or possess more than we need.

As we begin building our lives around him and become more knowledgeable of his will, we will be tested in many ways. We will sometimes pass and sometimes fail, and both are a part of our growth. Either way, we need to remember to restrain from pride, not thinking more highly of ourselves than others. God may be working differently with each of us, as our gifts differ according to our grace.

For through the grace given to me I say to everyone among you not to think more highly of himself than he ought to think; but to think so as to have sound judgment, as God has allotted to each a measure of faith. For just as we have many members in one body and all the members do not have the same function, so we, who are many, are one body in Christ, and individually members one of another. Since we have gifts that differ according to the grace given to us, each of us is to exercise them accordingly: if prophecy, according to the proportion of his faith; if service, in his serving; or he who teaches, in his teaching; or he who exhorts, in his exhortation; he who gives, with liberality; he who leads, with diligence; he who shows mercy, with cheerfulness.

Let love be without hypocrisy. Abhor what is evil; cling to what is good. Be devoted to one another in brotherly love; give preference to one another in honor. (Romans 12:3–10, NASB)

You may be thinking, "I am not a minister or teacher, and neither of these comes easy for me." But there are many ways to lead, and they are easily done with true love. As we know, testifying can sometimes be difficult, but we cannot become slack in serving the Lord.

Not lagging behind in diligence, fervent in spirit, serving the Lord; rejoicing in hope, persevering in tribulation, devoted to prayer, contributing to the needs of the saints, practicing hospitality.

Bless those who persecute you; bless and do not curse. Rejoice with those who rejoice, and weep with those who weep. Be of the same mind toward one another; do not be haughty in mind, but associate with the lowly. Do not be wise in your own estimation. Never pay back evil for evil to anyone. Respect what is right in the sight of all men. If possible, so far as it depends on you, be at peace with all men. Never take your own revenge, beloved, but leave room for the wrath of God, for it is written, "Vengeance is Mine, I will repay," says the Lord. "But if your enemy is hungry, feed him, and if he is thirsty, give him a drink; for in so doing you will heap burning coals on his head." Do not be overcome by evil, but overcome evil with good. (Romans 12:11–21, NASB)

God has chosen us, even though our love, understanding, and Fruits of the Spirit may be limited at times; we can always pray for knowledge, wisdom, and guidance while praying for one another.

(1 Timothy 2:1–4, NASB)

First of all, then, I urge that entreaties and prayers, petitions and thanksgivings, be made on behalf of all men, for kings and all who are in authority, so that we may lead a tranquil and quiet life in all godliness and dignity. This is good and acceptable in the sight of God our Savior, who desires all men to be saved and to come to the knowledge of the truth.

* * * * *

Testifying is not always easy, as we may not be able to find the right words or some may not believe or trust what you are sharing while others may not be ready. But I believe the best testimony we can share is begin an example of the Fruits of the Spirit, full of faith and love, while trying continually to overcoming the daily sinful natures we face.

Notes:

CHAPTER 7

Rest

Have you ever felt like you don't have enough time? Most of our lives are completely full to the point we wish we had more hours in a day, more days in a week, more weeks in a month, or more months in a year or more years in our life. At times, our lives become so consumed with our day-to-day activities that we lose sight of what's important. Balancing between families, work, physical, mental, spiritual, and emotional well-being is essential; therefore, we must allow ourselves to rest.

Resting in a biblical sense means to cease or abstain from our work. God is almighty and does not need rest, but he knew it was important. He demonstrated rest after creating the heavens and earth as example for us to live by.

(Genesis 2:1–3, NASB)

Thus the heavens and the earth were completed, and all their hosts. By the seventh day God completed His work which He had done, and He rested on the seventh day from all His work which He had done. Then God blessed the seventh day and sanctified it, because in it He rested from all His work which God had created and made.

* * * * *

God knew our daily lives would consume us, so he set aside and blessed the seventh day for us to be restored.

> "Jesus said to them, 'The Sabbath was made for man, and not man for the Sabbath'" (Mark 2:27, NASB).

This day was designed for us so that we could give ourselves a day of rest. While resting from our normal day to day schedules, we can reset our mind, feed our spirit, nourish our physical well- being, and serve others. This time is important to God, so important he commanded that it be kept throughout our generations and included it as one of the Ten Commandments.

> Remember the Sabbath day, to keep it holy. Six days you shall labor and do all your work, [10] but the seventh day is a Sabbath of the LORD your God; in it you shall not do any work, you or your son or your daughter, your male or your female servant or your cattle or your sojourner who stays with you. For in six days the LORD made the heavens and the earth, the sea and all that is in them, and rested on the seventh day; therefore the LORD blessed the Sabbath day and made it holy. (Exodus 20:8–11, NASB)

Today and in times past, for us to truly be able to honor this time, we must prepare for this day on weekly bases. If we do not prepare, we will find ourselves continuing to operate as we do daily.

> Then he said to them, "This is what the LORD meant: Tomorrow is a Sabbath observance, a Holy Sabbath to the LORD. Bake what you will bake and boil what you will boil, and all that is left over put aside to be kept until morning." (Exodus 16:23, NASB)

How many weekends have gone by without us truly taking the time to rest? Maybe we are not at work, but we're cutting grass, buying groceries, traveling from game to game, doing clothes, dishes etc. We then begin our work week completely drained, because we never gave ourselves time to renew, must less time to build on our relationship with the Lord. This becomes this whirlwind effect, and we become overwhelmed, stressed, irritable, selfish, and even spiteful to the ones we love, while growing distant in our relationship with him.

Resting does not mean staying in bed and sleeping all day, it is abstaining from our worries, chores, and work.

How satisfied do you feel when you have help someone, spent time in prayer, studied with the lord, your family, friends, or brethren? Jesus provides us many examples of how the Sabbath day should be fulfilled.

> At that time Jesus went through the grain fields on the Sabbath, and His disciples became hungry and began to pick the heads of grain and eat. (Matthew 12:1, NASB)

* * * * *

If we are hungry, we should feed our physical bodies, and if we see someone in need, we should be of service to them.

> And a man was there whose hand was withered. And they questioned Jesus, asking, "Is it lawful to heal on the Sabbath?" so that they might accuse Him. And He said to them, "What man is there

among you who has a sheep, and if it falls into a pit on the Sabbath, will he not take hold of it and lift it out? How much more valuable then is a man than a sheep? So then, it is lawful to do good on the Sabbath." Then He said to the man, "Stretch out your hand!" He stretched it out, and it was restored to normal, like the other (Matthew 12:10–13, NASB).

The Sabbath day is also a time to educate ourselves and teach others.

They went into Capernaum; and immediately on the Sabbath He entered the synagogue and began to teach. They were amazed at His teaching; for He was teaching them as one having authority, and not as the scribes. (Mark 1:21–22, NASB)

In addition to spiritual nourishment, we should also rest our bodies, having prepared for this day in order to properly do so. Remember, God created the Sabbath for us. It's our time to renew our souls, grow in our spirit, and refresh our physical bodies.

We have covered many different topics and have learned that evil is everywhere just waiting to deceive us. There are many opinions on these subjects, so I ask that you do not take my word or the word of others, but allow God to lead you to the truth.

"But examine everything carefully; hold fast to that which is good" (1 Thessalonians 5:21, NASB).

If we so desire, God will give us his Hold Spirit and write his laws in hearts. If we will just listen with faith in our heart, the Holy Spirit will guide us to the truth.

And the Holy Spirit also testifies to us; for after saying,

"This is the covenant that I will make with them. After those days, says the Lord, "I will put my laws upon their heart, and on their mind I will write them," He then says, "And their sins and their lawless deeds I will remember no more." (Hebrews 10:15–17, NASB)

God knew we were unable to earn our way into eternity with him, which is why he gave his only son as a sacrifice for us. When we truly walk with him, we will want to do the things that are pleasing to him, not to earn our way into heaven, but as a way of showing our love for him.

Trust in the LORD with all your heart
    And do not lean on your own understanding.
In all your ways acknowledge Him,
    And He will make your paths straight.
(Proverbs 3:5–6, NASB)

This book was written to touch and possibly revile the voids in our lives. God's word will take you much deeper that these seven simple chapters could ever do.

The information for this book has come from the New American Standard Bible, King James Version, The Strong's Concordances, research, and asking for God guidance.

To my knowledge, there is not a perfect translation from the oldest texts of God's words. As it is almost impossible to perfectly translate one language into another, especial with the time laps in its context and with today's English differing in grammar, as the words are not always synonymous with the original language. Slight differences in words and placement can lead you to believe the message in a different context. So again, I ask for you to follow God's guidance to the right material and understanding while growing in your relationship with him.

I hope this book has intrigued your interest enough to start or to continue on building your relationship with him. May God be with you and your journey with Him always.

I would like to extend a special thanks to my Lord and savior, family, friends, coworkers, and acquaintances, for your forgiveness, understanding, and guidance through my growth yesterday, today, and forever.

Notes:

CPSIA information can be obtained
at www.ICGtesting.com
Printed in the USA
LVHW041150180319
611004LV00006B/524/P